TRAPPED!

A Christian Murder Mystery

Georgianna Summers

Lima, Ohio
C.S.S. Publishing Company

TRAPPED! A Christian Murder Mystery

Copyright © 1984 by
The C.S.S. Publishing Company, Inc.
Lima, Ohio

2011/ISBN 0-89536-644-9 PRINTED IN U.S.A.

PRODUCTION NOTES

Stage Set:

This play can either be produced in a church sanctuary or on a stage. In a sanctuary, screens can be used for exits with a two- or three-step stair disappearing behind a screen to suggest the upstairs exit. The room should look warm and comfortable with a couch and/or overstuffed chairs, a fireplace, a telephone table with a chair by it, a free-standing coat rack, perhaps a green plant or two to suggest life, and any other furniture or properties to suggest a well-to-do atmosphere. Logs in the fireplace with an orange gel-covered light bulb behind them that can be screwed in or switched on when Josh lights the fire will add realism and warmth.

Properties:

On Stage — 3 hurricane lamps, telephone, candle in holder, matches, small logs piled next to fireplace

Offstage (kitchen) — large flashlight, candles, matches, small bowl and piece of bread, dishpan and towel

Offstage (upstairs) — house slippers

Josh — two sacks of groceries

Marie — suitcase, portable battery-powered radio/tape recorder

Jud — handgun

Dinah — purse with cosmetics, comb, mirror

Policeman — notebook and pen

Sound Effects:

Thunder, howling wind, loud crash, radio announcements on tape in radio/tape recorder (to be operated on stage as the radio), gun shot

Costumes and Make-up:

Josh — clean, neat cover-alls or jeans and flannel shirt, work jacket

Jim and John — dirty work clothes with fish blood on them, work jackets, fishing hats

Mr. Pharis — business suit, white shirt, tie, glasses, gray hair

Marie — pantsuit or casual dress and coat, befitting a middle-aged, middle class housewife. Hair up or short with a little gray

Jud — old clothes, old or leather jacket, unshaven, hair unkempt. Jacket wet

Dinah — sexy dress or pants and shirt, flashy jewelry, too much make-up. Should wear a wet raincoat on entrance

Hua — Ill-fitting dress from a thrift shop, old coat (wet), muddy, wet shoes. Black wig and Asian make-up

Policeman — dark slacks, khaki jacket, tan or brown shirt, plain dark tie

This play can either be given solely as a dramatic performance, as a worship service, or as a program with a discussion following. In any event, it would probably be helpful to include the following information on the printed program.

"This is not an ordinary whodunit. There are 'clues' throughout the play to help you discover the real meaning of the drama. Watch for them and the message. Here are some things to look for:
Who the characters really are. (Some of their names will give you a clue.)
Which lines and actions ring a bell.
How the main character is different from all the others.

WORSHIP SUGGESTIONS

Call to Worship: John 1:1-2, 4-5, 6-7, 14, 16-18

Hymn

Scripture:
It was now the day before the Passover Festival. Jesus and his disciples were at supper. After supper he said: "And now I give you a new commandment: love one another. As I have loved you, so you must love one another, then everyone will know that you are my disciples. The greatest love a person can have for his friends is to give his life for them. And you are my friends if you do what I command you. This then is what I command you: love one another." (Selected from John 13 and 15 — *Today's English Version*)

Announcement:
Because of the ending of the play, it is requested that there be no applause. Instead, we will sing Hymn No. _______________ "When I Survey the Wondrous Cross," without announcement.

Drama

Hymn:
"When I Survey the Wondrous Cross"

Benediction

TRAPPED!

(A Christian Murder Mystery)

The setting is the living room of a summer cottage in a wealthy area somewhere on the northeastern coast. It is a comfortable room with a fireplace, overstuffed chairs, tables, books, hurricane lamps. There are three exits — one to the outside, one to the kitchen, and one to the upstairs. As the play opens, the stage is dark. Josh, a young man in his early thirties, enters from the outside, carrying two sacks of groceries. He is followed by Jim, a strapping young man in his twenties, and his younger brother, John, who is high school age. As the outside door opens, the sound of thunder is heard.

JOSH: *(Calling over his shoulder.)* Come on in, guys, I'm glad you made it. *(Turns light switch on. Stage lights up.)*

JIM: *(Entering with **John**.)* Sorry we didn't make it earlier, Josh, but with this storm coming up it was hard to bring the boat in.

JOSH: No sweat, Jim. I decided to go on into town and get groceries. Hope you didn't have to wait too long. *(Puts sacks on table and takes his jacket off.)*

JIM: No, we just got here a few minutes before you did.

JOSH: Good. I'm glad we're all safely inside. Those clouds look like they're going to break any time. Here, you can hang your coats over here. *(Hangs his coat on a coat tree or wall hooks.)*

JOHN: *(Who has been taking it all in.)* Hey, this place is all right! But, boy, are we a mess. Fishing isn't the cleanest business in the world.

JIM: Or the best smelling.

JOSH: *(Picking up sacks.)* There's a bathroom in here off the kitchen and another one upstairs. You can both go clean up while I start supper. *(Exits to kitchen.)*

JIM: *(Calling to **Josh** offstage.)* We'll have to wait till Mom brings out our suitcase. It was so late we decided we'd better come straight here; so John called her from the dock. She should be here soon.

JOSH: *(Offstage)* What'ja do about your fish?

JIM: Dad took care of 'em. We didn't get too many today anyway.

JOHN: Josh, I wasn't sure if the electricity would be turned on; so I asked Mom to bring my transistor out so we could have a little music. Is that O.K.?

JOSH: Sure. But everything's working fine. Mr. King sent me the keys last week so I got the electricity, gas, and water turned on and the phone connected.

JOHN: *(Talking to **Jim**.)* This is sure a neat place. I never thought I'd get inside one of these fancy cottages on the south shore.

JIM: Me either. We're lucky to know Josh.

JOHN: Has he worked here long?

JIM: About three years, I think.

JOHN: What does he do?

JIM: Takes care of the place. Does the gardening, a little carpentry — you know — repairs things. Sort of a general — uh — servant in charge.

JOHN: Does this Mr. King live here all the time?

JIM: He's around, I think. (**Josh** *enters from kitchen.*)

JOHN: Are you sure it's all right for us to be here, Josh? After all, if you're only the caretaker —

JOSH: *(Starting to light fire in fireplace.)* Of course it's all right. In fact, Mr. King suggested it himself. Said, "Why don't you invite some of your friends over for a party before the season starts."

JOHN: He sounds like a great guy! *(Sound effects: wind howling.)*

JOSH: He is. The best! I'd sure like for you guys to meet him. In fact, once you meet him, I wouldn't be surprised if he offered *you* a job. He has lots of places that need looking after, and he's always looking for good help.

JOHN: All *right!* Would sure beat fishing for a living. *(Goes to window and looks out.)*

JIM: What's happened to Jud? I thought he was going to join us.

JOSH: I don't know. I invited him. He'll probably be along later.

JOHN: He'd better hurry before this storm breaks. Wind's getting bad.

JIM: Knowing Jud, he's probably hung up talking to somebody, trying to sign 'em up for his cause.

JOSH: *(Laughing)* You're probably right. Well, I need to check on things in the kitchen. Make yourselves at home. *(Pounding on front door.)* That sounds like Jud now. Would you guys get it? *(Exits to kitchen.)*

PHARIS: *(Offstage)* Open up in there, will you? (**Jim** *opens door.)* What's going on in here? Who are you? And what are you doing here?

JIM: *(Taken aback)* Well, I'm —

JOSH: *(Entering from kitchen.)* Oh, hello, Mr. Pharis.

PHARIS: *(Entering.)* Oh, it's you, Josh. What're you doing here? Season doesn't start till next week. And who are these fellows?

JOSH: These are my friends — Jim; his brother John. (**Jim** *starts to shake hands, but* **Pharis** *wrinkles up his nose at his dirty appearance and steps back.)* Mr. Pharis is a friend of Mr. King — I think.

PHARIS: What do you mean, you *think*? You know darn well I am. And I'm looking after his interests. I'm on my way into town for a meeting at the church, and when I saw the lights on, I thought I'd better investigate. There's so much lawlessness around these days, you never know.

JOSH: I appreciate your concern, Mr. Pharis. But it's really all right.

PHARIS: *(Suspiciously)* Does King know you're here with these — uh — friends?

JOSH: I assure you, Mr. Pharis, it's perfectly all right. You know I'm no lawbreaker. I've been taking good care of this place for three years. Mr. King sent me the keys last week to open up, and he suggested I invite some friends in for a party.

PHARIS: *(Doubtfully)* Well, I hope it's all right. *(Shaking his head and muttering as he starts to leave.)* That King — takes in everybody — I don't know —

MARIE: *(Opening front door)* Yoo-hoo! Anybody home? *(Sound effects: loud wind.)*

JOHN: Oh hi, Mom. Come on in.

MARIE: *(Closing door against the wind.)* Here's your suitcase. And your radio, John. That's quite a wind out there. I almost didn't make it in.

JIM: Mr. Pharis, this is our mother, Marie. She's brought us a change of clothes. You see, we've been out fishing all day. Our dad's a commercial fisherman. That's why we look so awful.

MARIE: *(Smoothing her hair down, anxious to make a good impression on someone like **Pharis**.)* How do you do? *(**Pharis** nods his head curtly.)*

JOSH: Won't you come in and sit down, Marie? Supper'll be ready soon.

MARIE: Thanks, Josh, but I think not. The weather's getting nasty out there, and I'd better get back into town before the storm breaks. Is it just going to be you four here for the week-end?

PHARIS: *(Indignant) I'm* not staying. In fact, I was just leaving.

JOSH: Mr. Pharis is a neighbor, Marie. He just stopped by for a minute. I've invited Jim and John and also Jud. He should be here any time.

MARIE: Jud! I wish I'd known that. H'mm. I'm not sure you should stay, John.

JOHN: *(Outraged)* Mom! For Pete's sake, quit treating me like a baby!

MARIE: Well, you're *not* very old, and I don't like you hanging around with people like Jud. It's all right for Jim because he's older, but you're so — so gullible.

PHARIS: *(Suspicious)* Who is this Jud? What's wrong with him? Look here, Josh, if you've invited in some —

JOSH: *(Trying to calm **Pharis**.)* He's all right, Mr. Pharis, believe me.

PHARIS: Well, Mrs. — er — ah — Marie doesn't think so.

MARIE: Oh, he's all right, I guess. It's just that he has some strange ideas, and some of his friends are — well, I just don't want my boys to get mixed up in any revolutionary scheme. Their father's doing well in the fishing industry, and they'll be taking over the business one of these days, and I —

PHARIS: Revolutionary! Now see here, Josh —

(Sound of a terrible crash. Lights go out.) Great Scott! What was that? (**Marie** *screams over* **Pharis's** *line.)*

JOHN: *(Excitedly)* The wind must have blown something over.

JOSH: Here, let me get a light. There's a candle here on the table — somewhere.

PHARIS: I hope whatever fell over didn't hit my car. That's all I need.

MARIE: Or mine. But we don't dare go out there to see.

JIM: Must have hit the power lines, too. (**Josh** *gets the candle lit. Stage lights come up a little.)*

JOSH: There's a flashlight in the drawer out in the kitchen. I'll get it. Maybe we can see what's happened outside. *(He exits to kitchen.)*

JIM: Why don't you turn your radio on, John? We may be having a hurricane.

MARIE: Oh, I hope not. We're awfully close to the beach here. (**John** *gets radio on.* **Jim, Marie,** *and* **John** *gather around and listen attentively.)*

RADIO VOICE: Police have issued an All Points Bulletin but all residents of the area are urged to stay inside with doors and windows locked. The murders are obviously the work of a madman or perhaps even a madwoman. At this point no one is sure. All we know is that it is extremely dangerous to be outside, not only because of the storm but because of the murders — three bodies found in the last hour in the immediate vicinity. *(Radio announcement continues as* **Marie** *and* **John** *say the next two lines. Static begins to come in.)* We repeat. Stay inside. Lock all doors and windows. Don't let anyone in. *(Static blurs out the rest.)*

MARIE: Is that our local station?

JOHN: Yeah. It's the only one we can get on this radio.

PHARIS: Can't even get *it* now. This dratted storm must be causing all that static.

JIM: Might as well turn it off. **(John** *does.)*

JOSH: *(Entering from kitchen.)* I found the flashlight. Maybe a couple of us can go out and see what damage has been done. *(Starts for door.)*

MARIE: *(Screaming)* Josh, don't open that door. Lock it!

JOSH: What?

JOHN: *(Excitedly)* It just came in on the radio. There's a murderer out there. He's already killed three people.

JOSH: Take that again, a little slower.

JIM: He's right. It just came in over his radio. They're saying to stay inside and keep all doors and windows locked.

MARIE: And not to let anyone in. It's dreadful, Josh. Some madman.

JOHN: Or woman. They don't know which. Lock the door.

JOSH: Well, okay, if you say so. I'll lock the front door. Jim, why don't you get the kitchen door. *(Goes to front door and locks it.)*

JIM: Got it. *(He leaves for kitchen.)*

JOSH: Here are some matches. Let's light the hurricane lamps and get some more light in here. *(Hands matches to **John** and **Marie**. He lights one lamp and they light the other two.)*

MARIE: *(Lighting lamp)* I hope your father's all right, John.

JOHN: *(Lighting lamp)* Yeah, me too. I hope he got home from the dock right away with this killer wandering around outside. *(Stage lights come up as the lamps are lit. **Jim** returns from kitchen.)*

JOSH: Now let's shine this flashlight through the window and see if we can see what's happened outside. *(They all gather around behind **Josh**.)* You're in luck, Mr. Pharis. It's a tree, but it missed your car.

MARIE: What about *my* car? Is it okay?

JOSH: Looks like it missed yours too, Marie.

MARIE: Thank goodness! *(She flops down on a chair in relief.)*

PHARIS: *(Who has pushed his way to the window.)* But we can't get out. It's blocked the driveway. Blast!

I'm supposed to be at that meeting at the church. I'll have to call 'em up. Where's the phone?

JOSH: Over there, Mr. Pharis, on the table. (**Pharis** *picks up phone and dials.)*

MARIE: You couldn't go anyway, Mr. Pharis. Not with that murderer out there.

PHARIS: That's a bunch of rubbish. Probably some Orson Welles' "War of the Worlds" thing. Now what? The phone's dead. That tree must have hit the telephone wires too. Blast! I never should have come in here. That's what I get for being concerned about someone else's property. I'll have to walk home now. *(He heads for the door.)*

MARIE: *(Rising)* Please, Mr. Pharis, don't go out there. The storm's too bad, and for all we know, that murderer could be in the front yard.

PHARIS: I told you, that's a bunch of nonsense. That could have been a soap opera, or one of those suspense programs.

JIM: That's true. We did turn it on in the middle of something, and then the static got so bad we didn't hear what came after. Three bodies *is* a little much. *(Pounding on front door.* **Marie** *screams.)*

JUD: *(Outside)* Hey, open up. Let me in quick. (**Josh** *goes to the door.)*

MARIE: *(Terrified)* Josh, don't open that door. They said not to let anyone in.

JOHN: Mom! Calm down. It was just a program.

(Pounding continues.)

JOSH: It's really okay, Marie. That sounds like Jud, and he's probably drenched. *(Opens the door and **Jud** stumbles in — soaking wet. Sound effects: rain.)*

JUD: What took you so long? I'm soaked.

JIM: You didn't walk all the way out from town?

JUD: No, I got a ride out with some friends, but they had to let me out at the road because of the tree that's blocking your driveway.

JOSH: Sorry about that, Jud. It just happened. The big question is, "What took *you* so long?" We've been waiting for you.

JUD: Don't you know? There's some insane person out there on the loose murdering people. The police have got all the roads blocked. All of us in the car had to give our life history in triplicate before they'd let us through. Stupid pigs!

MARIE: Then it *is* true. Quick, Josh, lock the door again.

JOSH: *(Locking the door.)* Well, it looks like we're going to have a bigger party than I planned for. But that's fine with me. You're all welcome. I'll just open up another can of stew. Stir up the fire, Jim, so Jud can dry out. All of you make yourselves at home. *(**Jim** works at fireplace. Jud takes off his coat and **Josh** hangs it up. **Pharis** keeps trying to get through on the phone.)*

MARIE: I think it's going to be an all-night siege,

Josh. Is there some room upstairs I can have?

JOSH: Of course. There are several bedrooms up there. Why don't you go up and take first pick. Here, take the flashlight. I think the one at the far end of the hall might be the most comfortable for you. *(She goes upstairs.)* Why don't you sit down and relax, Mr. Pharis. I'm sure they're not going to have that phone fixed for a while.

PHARIS: What are they going to think of me at the church? I'm the chairman of the meeting.

JOSH: I wouldn't worry about it. I'm going out to finish supper now. Maybe you could come help me, John. Bring the candle. We'll look for some more in the kitchen.

JOHN: Sure. *(They go out.* **Jud** *eyes* **Pharis** *suspiciously.)*

JUD: *(To* **Jim***)* Who's this guy?

JIM: Oh, I'm sorry. This is Mr. Pharis. He's a friend of Mr. King, Josh's boss. He just stopped by to — *(***Marie** *lets out a bloodcurdling scream from upstairs. Everyone jumps.* **Josh** *and* **John** *run in from the kitchen.)*

PHARIS: What now? My blood pressure can't stand much more.

JIM: *(Running up the stairs.)* Mom, what in the world —

MARIE: *(Staggering down the stairs, holding on to* **Jim***)* There's — a — a — man in the bedroom —

JOHN: The murderer!

MARIE: No — no — not the murderer. He's — he's been murdered. He's dead. *(She collapses in a chair.)*

JOSH: Dead? *(He starts up the stairs, followed by* **Jud, Jim,** *and* **John.***)*

MARIE: John, come back here.

JOHN: *(Coming back reluctantly)* Aw, Mom.

MARIE: You — you mustn't go up there. It's awful. He's lying on the bed. His throat's been cut. Blood everywhere.

PHARIS: The police. We've got to get the police. *(Runs to the phone)* Oh, Great Scott, we can't. *(Grabs his chest)* Oh, my heart. I'm gonna have a heart attack. I never should have come in here. *(***Jud** *returns. They all turn to him.)*

JUD: He's dead all right. Almost cut his head off. *(***Marie** *buries her head in her hands.)*

PHARIS: Do they know who he is?

JUD: *(Quietly)* Yes. *(Marie looks up.)*

PHARIS: And what in tarnation was he doing in this house? This is King's house. It was closed up, or at least I thought it was.

JUD: He's a relative of Josh.

MARIE: Oh no! A close one?

18

JUD: His cousin. *(**Josh** and **Jim** come down the stairs with their arms around each other. **Josh** sits. **Jim** stands behind him with his hands on his shoulders.)*

JOHN: Not John. *(**Jud** nods.)* Oh no!

MARIE: *(Going to **Josh**)* Josh, I'm so sorry. Jud just told us that he's your cousin. *(**Josh** nods with his head in his hands, trying to get control of his emotions.)*

JIM: He was a good man.

MARIE: You knew him?

JOHN: We all did.

MARIE: Who would have done such a thing — and why?

JUD: *(Bitterly)* I know why. He had a lot of enemies in the government. He wouldn't keep his mouth shut about their morals. The C.I.A. probably had a contract out on him.

PHARIS: The C.I.A.! Look here, what kind of an accusation is that? What are you — some kind of communist?

JOSH: Please! It's enough that he's been killed. Let's let the police find out who did it and why.

PHARIS: See here, Josh, this is a bad thing. I'm sorry.

JOSH: Thanks, Mr. Pharis. Thanks, all of you.

PHARIS: But what was he doing here? The place was all locked up. I checked yesterday.

JOSH: He had a key. He was a good friend of Mr. King's too. I didn't know he was here today. He must have been asleep upstairs when I unlocked this afternoon.

JOHN: How do we know when he was killed? Maybe he was already dead when you came today.

JIM: Or maybe he was killed while you were in town getting groceries.

MARIE: *(Petrified with terror)* Oh no! Maybe the murderer's still here — in the house.

JUD: She's right. We'd better search.

PHARIS: Look here, we can't do this unless we're armed. I don't have any weapon on me, and I don't think King keeps any firearms around the house.

JOSH: No, he doesn't.

JUD: I have a gun. *(Brings it out.)*

JOSH: *(Shocked)* Jud, what for?

JUD: What for? For this very reason. Obviously I'm the only one prepared. Come on, Jim — Pharis. Let's go upstairs and look around.

PHARIS: Well, I'm not sure —

JOHN: *(Eagerly)* I'll go.

MARIE: *(Sharply)* No, John, you're staying right here.

JOHN: Aw Mom, for Pete's sake!

JOSH: Stay with your mother, John. And you too, Mr. Pharis. I think we need to be cautious. I'll go with Jim and Jud. *(All three go upstairs.)*

MARIE: I can't believe this. We thought *we* were so safe inside here, and now —

PHARIS: You're not safe anywhere any more. No one respects the law. You can't trust anyone. You find that even the most law-abiding citizens cheat on their income tax, lie to their business partners. And this — this murderer that's loose, once they catch him — *if* they catch him — will just get a few years in prison and out he'll come again. I say to the gas chamber with all of them. A life for a life.

JOHN: But if the person's insane, shouldn't we try to help him? I mean —

PHARIS: Hogwash! Costs too much money. Besides — *(Knock on the front door)*

MARIE: *(Jumping)* Sh-sh-sh. What was that?

JOHN: It sounded like a knock on the door. *(Knock again)*

MARIE: It is. Oh, dear God, it's the murderer.

JOHN: Mom! Murderers don't knock on your door. I'll get it. *(Starts to door.)*

MARIE: John, don't!

PHARIS: Wait, young man. Your mother's right. I don't think we should let anybody in.

DINAH: *(Knocking and calling offstage.)* Hello? Is there anybody in there?

JOHN: It's a woman's voice. I'm not going to leave her standing out there in this storm. Besides, if we turn her away, the murderer could get her.

MARIE: You're right, John. As long as it's a woman, I think it's safe to let her in.

PHARIS: I don't know. They said on the radio they don't know if it's a man or a woman who's killed all those people. Let me handle this. *(Calls out)* What do you want?

DINAH: My car broke down. I think the engine's flooded. Please let me in to use your phone.

PHARIS: The phone's out because of the storm. You'd better go somewhere else.

JOHN: Mr. Pharis, for heaven's sake. It's raining out there, and she's alone and walking. Let her in.

MARIE: He's right. Let her in.

PHARIS: *(Reluctantly)* Well, all right. *(Opens the door)* Come on in. We've had quite a scare here, and we're being very cautious.

DINAH: *(Enters, wearing a dripping wet raincoat.)* Thanks. Was I ever glad to see your light. This is a helluva storm. That tree out there across your driveway is a big one.

MARIE: Come over here by the fire and take off your wet things. I'm sorry we were hesitant to let you in, but we've just had a terrible thing happen here, and we're all frightened to death.

DINAH: What happened?

JOHN: *(Dramatically)* Someone has been murdered upstairs.

DINAH: You're kidding!

PHARIS: We certainly are not, young lady. Marie here found him a few minutes ago in an upstairs bedroom with his throat cut. We don't know if the murderer's still here in the house; the phone is out, and we can't call for help. I hope you can see why we didn't want to let you in.

DINAH: Do you really think the murderer's still here?

MARIE: We don't know. Three of our men are upstairs now, looking around. Of course, he could be outside somewhere too. That's why we didn't want to leave you out there.

PHARIS: Where's your car?

DINAH: It's up the road a little ways. It completely died on me.

PHARIS: *(Suspiciously)* What are you doing out alone on a night like this?

DINAH: *(Bristling)* I don't think that's any of your business, Buster. (**Pharis** *gives her a look of utter disapproval.*)

MARIE: Didn't you hear the warning on the radio about the murderer? They cautioned everyone to stay inside.

DINAH: *(Still irritated)* No, I didn't. I didn't have the radio on.

PHARIS: *(Very suspicious)* Look, lady, if you've been out on the road, why weren't you stopped by the police? They've got all the roads blocked.

DINAH: *(Belligerent)* Well, they didn't have mine blocked. I just came from a couple of miles beyond here.

PHARIS: You don't look like a resident of this area to me. (*She gives him a dirty look as* **Jud, Josh,** *and* **Jim** *come back downstairs.*)

JOHN: *(Eagerly)* Did you find anything?

JOSH: No, there's no one up there.

MARIE: Thank God!

JOHN: Josh, Jim, Jud, this is — uh —

DINAH: Dinah.

JOHN: Her car broke down, and she came here to phone. Dinah, Josh is sort of the owner here.

JOSH: The caretaker. Glad to meet you, Dinah. I

guess they told you the phone's out, but you're welcome to stay.

JOHN: It was Josh's cousin that was murdered.

DINAH: I'm sorry.

JOSH: Thanks.

PHARIS: Well, tell us what you found out up there.

JOSH: Not much, Mr. Pharis. Look, I think I want to be alone for a few minutes. I'm going out to the kitchen to warm up some stew for us. Jud and Jim can fill you in on what we found upstairs. *(He leaves.)*

JOHN: Tell us. *(He and **Jud** sit down.)*

JIM: Well, actually we didn't find much of anything. We looked in all the rooms, under the beds, in the closets. There's no one up there.

MARIE: Did you go back in — in — *his* room?

JUD: Yeah. And it looks like he was killed here; that is, not like he was killed somewhere else and brought in.

PHARIS: Could you tell how recent?

JIM: Recent. Like right before we came or while we were down here talking. His body's still warm.

MARIE: Oh, dear God! How did the murderer get in?

JIM: Who knows? He could have had a key. He could have come in an unlocked window. There's a tree up there by the window that's easy to climb. He could have been someone John knew and maybe came here with him.

PHARIS: As a matter of fact, he could have been one of us.

JUD: Now look here, Pharis —

PHARIS: Well, just think of it. All we have is everybody's word. Josh says he was here earlier in the day, then he went into town to get groceries. Can he prove that?

JOHN: He drove up in the car with groceries right after we got here.

PHARIS: All right, but that doesn't tell you when he left. And you fellows — *(points to **Jim** and **John**.)*

JIM: We were out fishing all day. We told you. That's why we're so dirty.

PHARIS: But that's your story, and incidentally a perfect cover-up for a murder. Fish smell, fish blood — maybe. Who can verify it?

MARIE: Really, Mr. Pharis, this is the height of insult. I can verify it. They called me from the dock.

PHARIS: How do you know it was from the dock? And you, what were you doing all afternoon?

MARIE: Why I was — I don't have to answer that. This is preposterous.

PHARIS: Is it? And Jud — he arrives late. Where was he?

JUD: Look, man, I told you why I was late. Me and my friends went through all this with the police at the road block.

PHARIS: That's your story. We can't prove it. You could have been upstairs slitting that fellow's throat while we were all down here talking; then climbed down the tree and come around here and pounded on the door.

DINAH: This is rich. I think it's safer outside than in here.

PHARIS: And you, young woman, we don't know anything about you. You were out on the road, you said, but not stopped by the police. You could have been upstairs earlier, gone down the tree, waited outside until just now.

JUD: What about you, Pharis? What's your alibi?

JIM: That's right. We don't know what *you* were doing all afternoon. Since you and Mr. King are friends, you've probably got a key to the place. You could have killed him and then come back here all concerned about us being in here. Talk about a cover — solid citizen, going to a church meeting. The police would never suspect you.

PHARIS: *(Unperturbed)* Absolutely. See what I mean? Not one of us here has an air-tight alibi. It's just everybody's word, and as I said earlier, you can't trust anyone these days.

MARIE: This is ridiculous! You know it's bound to be that — that murderer out there, the one the radio said has murdered three other people.

PHARIS: If one of us is an insane murderer, we all had time to murder three other people before we came here.

JIM: He's right, you know.

JOSH: *(Entering from kitchen)* No, he isn't. He's wrong — dead wrong.

PHARIS: Since you're so sure, then I take it you know who did it and can prove it.

JOSH: No. But you're still wrong to spread distrust and suspicion among us. Yes, I heard it all from the kitchen. Look, we're here together — some willingly, others unwillingly — and we're unable to leave because of the circumstances. Temporarily grounded, so to speak —

PHARIS: *Trapped* is the word.

JOSH: As you like, Mr. Pharis. Anyway, we can either spend the night in terror, afraid that if we close our eyes or turn our backs someone among us will slit our throats, or we can trust each other and spend the night in fellowship as friends and companions. Frankly, I prefer the latter.

JOHN: I'm with you, Josh.

DINAH: Right on!

PHARIS: Sentimental nonsense, if you ask me. Better to be cautious than foolish. *(Knock on front door.)*

MARIE: *(Jumping)* Oh no! Someone else out there. Jud, quick, get your gun! **(Jud** *rushes to door with his* *gun drawn.)*

JOSH: *(Following him)* Put that thing away, Jud. I'm still the host here. *(Calls)* Who is it?

HUA: *(Speaking with Vietnamese accent in broken English.)* Mitter King?

JOSH: He isn't here right now. This is Josh, his caretaker. What do you want?

HUA: I want Mitter King, please.

PHARIS: Send her away, Josh. This may be a trap.

JUD: He's right. She could be working with the murderer.

PHARIS: *(Yelling)* He's not here, lady. Go away.

JOSH: Quiet, Pharis. *(Calling through door.)* What is it you want?

HUA: Use phone. Call doctor. Lit-tle girl very sick. Mitter King help.

PHARIS: She's some foreigner. She'll never understand.

JIM: We really can't help her, Josh, since our phone is out. Tell her to go somewhere else.

DINAH: Hey, look, you let *me* in. Are you gonna leave *her* out there to be killed?

PHARIS: She's different. She's not one of us. And I think we're pushing our luck to let another stranger in.

MARIE: That's true, Josh. You're responsible for all of *us*. You don't need to take *her* on.

JOSH: *(Torn)* I'm sorry, Ma'am. Our phone is out of order. Maybe the next house down the road can help you.

HUA: *You* help me. Mitter King help me. Lit-tle girl very sick.

JOSH: She's not going to go away. I can't leave her out there. I'm going to let her in. *(He opens the door and* **Hua** *stumbles in.)*

HUA: *(Looking around at group.)* Mitter King? You know Mitter King?

JOSH: Yes, I know him. I work for him.

HUA: He my friend. Bring my family here — to this country.

JOSH: Oh. I see. He was your sponsor. *(She nods.)* Come on over to the fire.

HUA: *(Grabbing his hand.)* Call doctor. My lit-tle girl very hot. Talk funny.

MARIE: Sounds like she's delirious with fever.

PHARIS: Look, lady, we can't call a doctor. *(Goes to phone and takes it off the hook.)* Here, see — phone, no work. Tree outside fall down, hit line. *(He pantomimes.)*

HUA: *(Looking confused and turning to* **Josh**.*)* You help me? You come?

JOSH: I'm sorry. I have to take care of these people here. Look, Mrs. — what is your name?

HUA: My name Hua. *(Pronounced Whah.)*

JOSH: Look Hua, you stay here. *(Pantomime)* Soon, maybe, the phone will work again. Then we call doctor.

HUA: My lit-tle girl very sick.

JOSH: *(Compassionately)* I know.

JOHN: Is she alone? (**Hua** *doesn't understand.*)

MARIE: Is your husband with her?

HUA: My husband work. Not home.

DINAH: Then the kid *is* alone.

HUA: My big girl with her.

MARIE: Good. Come sit down, honey. We'll get some help soon.

JOSH: Look — supper is ready. I think we should eat.

JUD: Good idea. I'm starved.

JOSH: We'll have to eat in shifts because there isn't room around the kitchen table for all of us at the same time. Let's have the ladies first, and you can join them, Jud, since you're so hungry.

JOHN: Hey, I'm starved too. I should have spoken up first. It's not fair. It looks like those who came last are gonna be served first, and those of us who came first are gonna be last.

JOSH: *(Laughing)* It kind of looks that way, doesn't it?

MARIE: You can have my place, dear, if you're so hungry.

JIM: He's always hungry, Mom. He can wait. We had a hamburger at the dock before we came out here; so he's not starving. And I'll bet *you* didn't have anything before you came out.

MARIE: Well, no, I didn't. I was going to fix supper for your dad when I got back. Little did I know I'd be stuck here all night. Come to think of it, I *am* hungry.

JOSH: Well, come on out, you four. *(To **Hua**)* Come, we go eat. *(Pantomimes eating as they go out to the kitchen.)*

PHARIS: *(Grumbling)* Little did I know *I'd* be stuck here all night either. What a mess. Let's turn on the radio again and see if we can get anything.

JOHN: Probably can't. *(Turns it on.)*

RADIO VOICE: *(Static)* — In the last hour two more bodies have been found in the south shore area. From their clothing it is obvious that all of the victims have been poor or working class individuals, several of them minorities, a strange circumstance since they have been found in the south shore area which is noted for its expensive homes. Police are surmising that they are domestics who work for the wealthy residents in the area. So far the police still have no clues as to the murderer's identity, although footprints around the bodies appear to be small which leads to the speculation that the murderer could be a woman. However, Police Chief Caifus notes that heavy rains and muddy ground have obliterated most of the prints, making it impossible to determine the exact size. Because of the extreme danger, the Chief of Police had issued the following directive: No one is to be out on the streets or roads. Anyone who goes outside will be stopped by the police or quite possibly be mistaken for the murderer and shot. I repeat — no one is to go outside. Also, the police are speculating on the possibility that the murderer or murderess may have sought shelter in someone's home. Therefore, do not let anyone whom you do not know into your house. He or she could be the murderer. *(Radio starts to run down.)* I repeat — do not let anyone into your home —

PHARIS: What's happening? Turn it up.

JIM: Sounds like the batteries are gone. Did you ask Mom to bring some replacements, John?

JOHN: No. I didn't know they were about gone. Geez!

PHARIS: Well, that's just great.

JOHN: Where's that flashlight? Let me see if those batteries will fit. *(Gets flashlight and tries the batteries in the radio during the next lines.)*

PHARIS: Just what I thought. Either one of those two women we've let in could be the murderer. You heard what they said — small footprints. I knew we shouldn't have let them in. That foreign woman — she doesn't have the money to live around here.

JIM: If Mr. King sponsored them, maybe he's provided a house for them.

PHARIS: I don't think there's a word of truth in her story. Look how she wouldn't go away. She knew the police were all around and she had to get inside. All that trumped-up story about a sick child. And pretending she doesn't understand English. A perfect alibi. We're harboring a murderer, I just bet. *(To* **John***)* Do those batteries fit?

JOHN: No — too big.

PHARIS: Well, I'm going outside to see if I can flag down a policeman. They can take both of these women in, and then they can take *me* home. *(Starts for door.)*

JIM: I wouldn't do that, Mr. Pharis. Remember they said on the radio that you could be shot. No one is to go outside.

PHARIS: *(Livid)* Blast it all! We're trapped! Trapped like mice in a cage. **(Marie** *and* **Dinah** enter, engaged in conversation. **Hua** *follows and heads for the phone.)*

MARIE: *(Hotly)* I don't see anything wrong in looking after your family. I'm proud of my boys, and I love my husband, and I'm happy to look after them.

DINAH: Yeah, well I'm looking after number one. **(Josh** *enters and starts talking to* **John** *while the following conversation between the three women is carried on in the background around the phone.)*

HUA: *(Picking up phone)* Call doctor.

MARIE: *(Taking phone from her)* It's still dead. *(To* **Hua***)* Phone still not work.

DINAH: *(Pantomiming action)* Phone dead. Line cut by big tree. (**Hua** *sits in chair by telephone table and puts her head in her hands, crying.* **Marie** *tries to comfort her.*)

JOSH: Well, John, if you aren't too weak from hunger, maybe you can crawl out to the kitchen, and I'll serve you and Jim and Mr. Pharis some supper now.

JOHN: *(Holding his stomach in mock starvation.)* I'll never make it. *(Exits)*

PHARIS: I'm not hungry. I ate before I stopped by here. (**Jud** *enters with a bowl in which he's sopping out the last of the stew with a piece of bread*).

JIM: Well, why don't you at least come out and have a glass of wine with us. You can tell Josh about your concern. *(Nods at* **Hua***.* **Josh** *follows* **John** *into the kitchen.)*

PHARIS: Somebody needs to keep an eye on things in here. *(Quietly to* **Jud***)* Have you still got that gun?

JUD: *(Patting his pocket)* Right here. (**Jim** *leaves, shaking his head.*)

PHARIS: Good. Keep an eye on that Jap woman.

JUD: *(Giving him a dark look)* She's Vietnamese.

PHARIS: Whatever. Also the other one. *(Nods toward* **Dinah** *as he follows* **Jim** *out.)*

DINAH: What was that all about?

JUD: Oh, you know Pharis. Suspicious of everyone who isn't exactly like him. I hate his kind.

DINAH: So do I. Typical male chauvinist. I'd hate to be his wife.

MARIE: You really hate men, don't you?

DINAH: Honey, I love men. But I don't let 'em interfere with my life. I do the choosing, and I do the leaving. I don't work for anybody but me.

JUD: Ever join a cause?

DINAH: What for? People who join causes are out for power. I'm not into power.

MARIE: What are you into?

DINAH: I told you. I'm into doing what feels right for me. *(Gets out her purse and starts putting on make-up, filing her nails, combing her hair, etc.)*

HUA: *(Turning to* **Marie.***)* Please, my lit-tle girl. She die. Get doctor. *(She heads for the front door.)*

MARIE: *(Running to stop her.)* You mustn't go out there. Bad man. Slit throat. *(Pantomimes)* Stay here. *(Brings her back to the chair.)*

HUA: *(Crying)* My lit-tle girl. She die. **(Marie** *cuddles her.)*

MARIE: *(To* **Dinah***)* Look, *she* isn't into doing what just feels right for *her*. She doesn't care about herself.

She wants to save her child. Poor thing. I understand that. I'd do anything for my boys.

JUD: What about other people's boys? *(To* **Dinah***)* All you care about is yourself. *(To* **Marie)** All you care about is your family. My Liberation Party cares about all the people who're dying from the oppression of the rich. That's why I hate guys like Pharis — big business executives and pillars of the church — skinning the poor to line their own pockets.

MARIE: You can't save the world, Jud. All you can do is look after your own.

JUD: Saving the world *is* looking after your own. Look, Marie, how long do you think your husband's little fishing business is going to last in our corporation society? One of these days Pharis, or someone like him, is going to offer to buy it, and if he refuses to sell, his corporation, which is a subsidiary of God knows how many other corporations, will undersell him and run him out of business.

MARIE: *(Disgusted)* Oh, Jud, that's not true. People like Mr. Pharis are all for free enterprise. They're good Americans.

JUD: *(In utter disgust)* Oh brother! How naive can you get? They could care less for America. Most of their money is tied up in multi-national corporations. They'd sell out to anybody for the almighty dollar.

PHARIS: *(Shouting from kitchen)* I don't believe you, Josh. That's a blasphemous lie! Why didn't King tell *me?* I'm his friend.

MARIE: I wonder what Mr. Pharis is so upset about?

JUD: Who cares? He's always upset.

PHARIS: *(Entering, muttering in outrage)* That's outrageous! I don't believe it.

DINAH: *(Sarcastically)* Had a little argument, did you? Sounds like maybe you and this fellow King aren't as good friends as you thought.

PHARIS: Oh, shut up!

DINAH: *(Standing and facing him belligerently)* Look here, Buster, no one tells *me* to shut up. **(Josh** *enters, followed by* **John** *and* **Jim.)**

JOSH: I think we've all got frayed nerves from the circumstances of the evening. From what you tell me was on the radio, it looks like we're going to be here all night; so why don't we get settled down for some good rest.

MARIE: I couldn't shut my eyes for one minute.

HUA: *(Going to* **Josh)** Mitter King's friend. Call doctor, please.

JOSH: Has anyone checked the phone? **(John** *picks it up.)*

JOHN: Still dead.

JOSH: Marie, why don't you take Hua upstairs away from all these people. I think maybe you could make her understand if you were with her alone, and then give her some support and comfort until we can get through to a doctor.

MARIE: I don't want to go near that room where — where the body is.

JOSH: We locked the door. No one can go in there. There are several other bedrooms, you know.

MARIE: All right. Come, Hua, we go upstairs. (*As they start to leave,* **Josh** *notices* **Hua's** *feet.*)

JOSH: Wait, Marie, look at this poor woman's feet. Her shoes are sopping wet and muddy. She must have walked across the field to get here.

PHARIS: Aha!

JOSH: She'll catch her death. John, would you please go out to the kitchen and get that pan of warm water I fixed to wash dishes in? And bring a towel. Here, Hua, let's sit down a minute and get these wet shoes off. (*He sits her down, removes her shoes. John returns with the water, and Josh washes her feet and dries them during the next few lines.*)

DINAH: Wow! You sure take this business of being the caretaker very seriously, don't you?

JOSH: Yes, as a matter of fact, I do. But then, of course, I would hope all of us would be caretakers. Perhaps you could go upstairs to the first bedroom on the right, Dinah, and look in the closet. I think there are some warm slippers there.

DINAH: Sure.

JIM: I'll go with you, since you aren't familiar with the house. Where's the flashlight? (*Someone gives it to him, and they go upstairs.*)

JOHN: I'll go out and get some candles from the kitchen so we can all have lights in our rooms.

JOSH: Good thinking, John. Thanks. (**John** *leaves.*)

JUD: *(Yawning)* I'm tired. I'm gonna turn in. Where shall I sleep?

JOSH: Take your pick. All the rooms except — that one are available.

MARIE: Is there heat up there and comfortable beds?

JOSH: The front bedroom has a gas heater, and the beds in there are probably the best.

MARIE: Then can Jim and John have that one, Josh? After all, they were the original invited guests before all the rest of these people came.

JUD: Hey, how about me? I was invited too.

MARIE: *(Ignoring **Jud**)* They can have it, can't they, Josh?

JOSH: It isn't for me to say which room they can have, Marie. It's Mister King's house. (**Jim** *and* **Dinah** *return with slippers for* **Hua.** **John** *returns from kitchen with a box of candles and matches. He stands at the foot of the stairs to hand lighted candles to those who go upstairs.*) Thanks, Dinah. Here Hua, put these on. We'll put your wet shoes here by the fire to dry.

PHARIS: Leave 'em there. The police may want to check them.

40

JOSH: *(Firmly)* Mr. Pharis, that's enough about that. Come, Hua, Marie will take you upstairs. I'll check the phone throughout the night and let you know.

JOHN: *(Handing **Marie** a lighted candle.)* Here, Mom. **(Marie** and **Hua** go upstairs.)

JOSH: Well, what do the rest of you want to do?

DINAH: I guess I'll turn in. **(John** hands her a candle as she goes upstairs.)

JIM: What are *you* going to do, Josh?

JOSH: I'm going out to the kitchen to clean up.

JOHN: We'll help you, won't we, Jim?

JIM: Sure.

JOSH: Thanks. I'll give you guys a good recommendation if you ever want my job. Well, Jud and Mr. Pharis, there are rooms available upstairs if you want to turn in.

PHARIS: I'm staying right here.

JOSH: Suit yourself. **(Josh, Jim** and **John** exit to kitchen. One of them takes the pan of water. **Jud** lights a candle and starts upstairs.)

PHARIS: Jud?

JUD: Yeah? What do *you* want?

PHARIS: Do you still have that gun?

JUD: Yes. Why?

PHARIS: I'd like to borrow it.

JUD: What for?

PHARIS: I have reason to believe that one of those two women who came in here with their stories may be the murderer. And also I'm very suspicious of Josh after that preposterous lie he told me at supper.

JUD: What lie?

PHARIS: Never mind. I just think it's wise to be cautious. While you were eating supper, those of us out here got the radio to work for a few minutes. The police think the murderer could well be taking shelter in someone's home out here on the south shore. They said not to let any strangers in and not to let anyone go out.

JUD: Have you told Josh?

PHARIS: Yes — for what it was worth. He wouldn't listen. He has a total disregard for the law. You can see how he just went ahead and let that — that Vietnamese woman in.

JUD: What are you gonna do with the gun?

PHARIS: Nothing, unless I need to. But I want to keep guard down here in case anyone tries anything.

JUD: I don't know.

PHARIS: I'll pay you for the loan of it, just for tonight.

JUD: Yeah? How much?

PHARIS: How about — uh — $20.00?

JUD: Well, I don't —

PHARIS: *(Quickly)* Thirty!

JUD: H'm. I could use it for my organization's treasury. Understand, I don't like taking money from guys like you, Pharis. But if you want to contribute to the People's Liberation Party, that's your business. You're sure you're not gonna shoot anybody.

PHARIS: No. I just want it for everybody's safety. Here's your money. *(Gives him the $30.00. **Jud** hands over the gun.)*

JUD: Thanks, Mr. Pharis. The people will rise because of you. *(Takes a lighted candle and goes upstairs. **Pharis** moves around the room turning down the hurricane lights. Stage lights go down simultaneously so that the stage is lit only by the hurricane lamps, the candle that was lit when the lights first went out, and the light from the fireplace. **Pharis** sits down by the fire. After about ten seconds, **Hua** comes stealing down the stairs and goes to the fireplace to get her shoes.)*

PHARIS: *(Jumping up)* Ha! Just as I thought. Going out to murder someone else. *(Pulls the gun.)* Hold it right there. (**Hua** *screams.* **Josh** *runs in from the kitchen, followed by* **Jim** *and* **John**.)

JOSH: Mr. Pharis, what are you doing?

PHARIS: I'm stopping this murderer from going out to kill someone else. She just sneaked down here to get her shoes.

HUA: *Turning to* **Josh***)* I go for doctor. My lit-tle girl, she die. *(Others from upstairs come rushing down and gather around.)*

JOSH: Pharis, put that gun away. You're frightening her and everybody else to death. Somebody turn the lights up. *(Those nearest the lamps turn them up. Stage lights come up full simultaneously.)* Come on, Mr. Pharis, let me have the gun.

PHARIS: No! Stand back, all of you. *(He holds them all at bay with the gun.)* Someone here is the murderer, and I don't intend to let them escape from the law.

JOSH: You're the murderer, Pharis. This poor woman here is trying to save the life of her daughter, and you won't let her. She was only trying to go out for a doctor.

MARIE: But she can't go out there, Josh. It's too dangerous.

JOHN: That's right, Josh. We told you about the radio announcement. All the victims have been poor people and minorities. She's a perfect target.

HUA: Please. I must go. Wait too long. My lit-tle girl die.

JIM: Somebody try the phone. Maybe it's fixed. *(Whoever is nearest the phone picks it up and responds: "Still dead.")*

JOSH: There's only one thing to do. I'm going.

JOHN: You can't go out there, Josh. It's too dangerous.

44

MARIE: Don't go, Josh. They'll get you.

JIM: We need you here. Wait till morning.

JOSH: That may be too late. I must go now. Out of my way, Mr. Pharis.

PHARIS: No. You can't break the law again, Josh. I won't let you.

JOSH: What law?

PHARIS: I told you what they said on the radio. The police chief has said that no one is to go out on the street. Anyone who does will be stopped or quite possibly be mistaken for the murderer and shot. You and your friends have already broken the law twice tonight by letting in these two women whom you don't know and exposing us all to unknown danger. You have got to be stopped!

JOSH: I'm sorry, Mr. Pharis, but you can't stop me. There's a child dying, and we can't make Hua understand why we can't help her. The only way we can make her understand that we care is for one of us to go.

JOHN: But why does it have to be you, Josh? Why can't Mr. Pharis go?

PHARIS: I'm not going. Why should I risk my life for this woman, who for all we know may be the murderer?

JOSH: Why indeed, Mr. Pharis? No, I'm the one to go. I'll try to flag down a policeman and get a ride into town. Maybe they can even radio ahead to a doctor and come back here and take Hua home to her children. And they can take all of you who want to leave, home.

JIM: But they may mistake you for the murderer and shoot you, Josh.

JOSH: They know me. They've seen me around here for the past three years. So don't be afraid. I'll go, and you won't need to be trapped here any more. *(To* **Hua.***)* I go get doctor for you. *(She grabs his hand in gratitude.)* Jim and John, take care of things here till I come back. Please put the gun away, Mr. Pharis. It's the spirit of the law that needs to be enforced, and that's done by the heart and not by the gun. *(He takes his jacket and walks out.)*

PHARIS: He's a fool! I won't let him do it. *(Goes out door, yelling)* Come back here, Josh. *(Offstage)* Stop him, someone. Help, Police, stop that man!

DINAH: They'll both be shot.

JUD: No they won't. Guys like Pharis never get it.

JOHN: That's the truth!

JIM: We never should have let Josh go out there.

DINAH: It's Pharis we should have stopped. *(Sound of shot.)*

MARIE: Oh, dear God, what was that?

JOHN: It sounded like a shot. I'll bet Pharis shot Josh.

46

JUD: I never should have let him have my gun.

JIM: Why did you?

JUD: He offered me $30.00 to borrow it. I took the money for my Liberation Party. I didn't think Josh would let him use it.

HUA: What happen?

MARIE: We don't know, Hua.

DINAH: Maybe Pharis just shot in the air. *(Knock on door.)*

JIM: I'll get it. *(Goes to door.)* Who's there?

POLICEMAN: *(Offstage)* Police. Please open up. (**Jim** *opens the door.)*

JIM: Yes, Officer, can we help you?

POLICEMAN: We've just shot a man. A gentleman named Mr. Pharis said he lived here.

MARIE: Oh no — Josh! Is he — is he — dead, Officer?

POLICEMAN: I'm afraid so, Ma'am. *(Everyone responds in stunned horror.)*

JIM: Come in, Officer. (**Policeman** *enters.)*

JOHN: *(Tearfully)* Why did you shoot him?

POLICEMAN: We thought he was this murderer that's running loose. We heard someone shout, "Stop that man," so we shot.

JUD: *(Bitterly)* Pharis! Here's his filthy money! *(Throws the $30 on the floor)* *(Sobbing)* I don't want it! I could kill myself for ever taking it!

JOHN: *(Emotionally)* He was no murderer — no law-breaker. He went out there to find a doctor for this lady's little girl. *(Sobbing)* He was the kindest, most caring man I ever knew.

JIM: *(Putting his arm around **John**.)* He went out there for all of us. Pharis was right. We *were* trapped in here — frightened, suspicious, thinking only of ourselves. And in a sense, each of us was the murderer. We should have all gone with him. Then whoever or whatever was out there wouldn't have had the power to overcome us. But we didn't. We let Josh go for us.

POLICEMAN: What did you say his name was? *(Starts writing his report.)*

JIM: Josh — Joshua.

POLICEMAN: Joshua who?

JIM: King.

MARIE: King! Then he was —

JIM: That's right. He told John and me and Pharis at supper. Pharis didn't believe him, but it's true. He was Mr. King's son.

(Everyone freezes in shocked silence as the curtain slowly closes. If there is no curtain, there should be a brief pause. Then as the lights go slowly down, the policeman turns and exits out the front door. Jud goes

up the stairs. Marie puts her arm around Hua, and they go out the front door, followed by Dinah. Jim and John exit to the kitchen. All exits should be made slowly, in the attitude of mourning.)

DISCUSSION SUGGESTIONS

1. Who do you think the characters were?

Biblical Reference	**Incident in Play**
Josh John 13:4-5, 12-17 John: 15:12-15	Washed Hua's feet. Told Dinah he hoped they all would be caretakers. Gave his life to save Hua's child and to free everyone who was trapped in the house. His last three speeches. Other clues: Joshua — another name for Jesus. Mr. King's son. Is a servant.
Jim and John Matthew 4:21-22	Fishermen, sons of fisherman. Close friends of Josh.
Marie Matthew 20:20-28	Wants her boys to have the best room. Josh's response.
Jud Matthew 26:14-15	Came from kitchen sopping his bread in a dish. Sold his gun to Pharis for $30. Was a zealot for his cause. Hated the establishment. Was treasurer for his organization. Threw his money down; wished to kill himself.
Pharis Luke 18:9-14 Mark 14:61-64	Loyal church member. Despised everyone not like him. Law very important to him. Looked after King's interests. Wouldn't believe that Josh was King's son.

50

Dinah
John 8:1-11

Obviously a lady of the street; loved men; cared only about herself. Her name means "judged."

Hua
Matthew
15:21-28

Was a foreigner. Wouldn't be turned away. Little girl was sick.

Policeman
Luke 23:24-24

Killed Josh at the command of Pharis.

The murdered man upstairs
Matthew
14:3-13

Josh's cousin. Had a lot of enemies in the government. Wouldn't keep his mouth shut about their morals. Friend of Mr. King's too.

2. Who was Mr. King?

3. Who was the murderer? Do you agree or disagree with Jim's statement at the end — "In a sense, each of us was the murderer, etc." How do we kill people? If everyone followed Josh's (Jesus's) way, then would the world be a safe, happy place?

www.ingramcontent.com/pod-product-compliance
Lightning Source LLC
Chambersburg PA
CBHW050627070726
47592CB00028B/1740